D0236330

The Concorde Story

The Concorde Story

Peter R. March

Sutton Publishing

Sutton Publishing Limited
Phoenix Mill, Thrupp, Stroud
Gloucestershire, GL5 5BU

First published 2005

British Library Cataloguing in Publication Data
A catalogue for this book is available from the British Library.

ISBN 0-7509-3980-X

Typeset in 9.5/14.5 Syntax
Typesetting and origination by
Sutton Publishing Limited.
Printed and bound in England by
J.H. Haynes & Co. Ltd, Sparkford.

ACKNOWLEDGEMENTS

In compiling what is essentially a photographic tribute to the legendary Concorde I must thank at the outset all those talented photographers who have recorded the production and flight of this beautiful airliner and are sharing these magnificent images with us here.

The late Arthur Gibson photographed Concorde in many different locations around the world and produced some enduring classics, as have the company and airline photographers on both sides of the Channel. Dave Charlton/Aerospace Imaging has provided access to many of these and the photo libraries originally established by the Bristol Aeroplane Company and its successors, through the British Aircraft Corporation, British Aerospace and Airbus UK at Filton. The former Bristol Siddeley Engines/Rolls-Royce photo library at Patchway also contributed a number of early images.

I am grateful to Gordon Bartley, Peter Cooper/Falcon Aviation Photos, Richard Cooper, David Donald/AIRTime Publishing Inc and my sons Andrew and Daniel March who have all contributed a number of exceptional images.

I have been ably assisted in producing the narrative and chronology of Concorde's three and a half decades by Edwin Shackleton and Brian Strickland. I would also like to thank Oliver Dearden of the Bristol Aero Collection for his kind help with this pictorial record.

Photo credits

Photographs Airbus UK/Aerospace Imaging unless otherwise credited.

There are a number of memorable aircraft of the first century of powered flight, as the development of flying machines progressed from fragile flimsy single-seaters to streamlined supersonic airliners. The piston-engined wood and canvas biplanes of the early years to the stealthy sophisticated jet bombers and fighters today, not forgetting helicopters, vertical take-off and landing jets and space shuttles on the way, have all produced their icons. When Concorde, the first successful super-sonic passenger airliner, joined that list in 1969, few people would have expected it to be consigned to history before the centenary of powered flight was reached on 17 December 2003.

In September 1949 I saw the mighty Bristol Brabazon climbing slowly out of Filton Airfield, Bristol on its maiden flight and, following it into the air three years later, the graceful Bristol Britannia – the Whispering Giant. Two decades after the ponderous Brabazon took off, I was again at Filton for the exhilarating noise and excitement of the British-built Concorde taking to the sky for its first flight to Fairford. These joyful moments in my years enthu-siastically following the aviation scene in Bristol were over-come by sadness on 26 November 2003. Shortly after 1 p.m. on a cold and showery late autumn day, Concorde 216/G-BOAF touched down at Filton at the end of the last ever flight by the supersonic airliner. It was particularly poignant that this aircraft, the last of the type to be built and fly from Filton on 20 April 1979, was returning home.

It was this emotional experience that convinced me that I should compile an inexpensive yet comprehensive photographic tribute to this twentieth-century techno-logical masterpiece that was part designed, built and first flown from my local airfield. As I write this intro-duction a year on from 216's last flight I mourn the loss of the familiar sight and sound of Concorde flying high over my home as it headed out over the West Country en route to New York. Every time I fly my light aircraft from Filton I see Concorde 216 sitting gracefully in the Airbus/Bristol Aero Collection compound and wish that the clock could be turned back to see the beautiful bird

in its rightful place in the sky. Realistically I know this is not going to happen and I have to be content with my photo, video and CD memories and of course make visits to the Concordes preserved in museums and collections.

I hope that you enjoy this souvenir of the legend that was Concorde – one of the great machines of the twentieth century and certainly the most beautiful flying machine of all time.

Peter R. March
Bristol
26 November 2004

The development of the jet engine more than sixty years ago, before the Second World War began, led to the development of the world's first jet warplanes that by the late 1940s became capable of flying faster than the speed of sound, at least in a dive. In Britain the world's first jet airliner, the de Havilland Comet, entered service with BOAC and in the USA the Boeing 707 and Douglas DC-8 were soon attracting orders from the world's major airlines. As a result transatlantic jet passenger services, which commenced on 4 October 1958, saw much shorter flight times and the thoughts of designers turned towards the possibility of supersonic air travel.

The word 'supersonic' describes the flight of an aircraft at a speed greater than the speed at which sound travels. The actual speed of sound can vary quite considerably, according to the air pressure and temperature, so it is quite different down at sea level than at 60,000 feet. A Mach number (named after Austrian physicist Ernst Mach) is used to describe the speed of an aircraft as a ratio of the speed of sound, with Mach 1 being the point after which the aircraft is 'supersonic'. Therefore an aircraft travelling at Mach 2 will be flying supersonic at twice the speed of sound.

In the early 1950s Sir Arnold Hall, who was then director of the Royal Aircraft Establishment (RAE) at Farnborough, started a study into the problems of supersonic travel. In 1954 the committee of which he was a member reported favourably. Two years later, on 5 November 1956, Morien Morgan was appointed chairman of the Supersonic Transport Aircraft Committee (STAC), within the Ministry of Aviation. This included representatives from the airlines, aircraft industry and

CONCORDE THE LEGEND

"Concorde was born from dreams, built with vision and operated with pride. Concorde has become a legend today."

Captain Mike Bannister, speaking to the passengers aboard the last scheduled Concorde flight from New York to Heathrow

At Filton, Bristol the British Concorde G-BSST is seen nearing completion in 1968, with part of the first production aircraft G-AXDN alongside.

ministries. Another three-year study finally came to the conclusion, in 1959, that supersonic airline flight was both practical and feasible, but the cost of its development would be completely beyond the capability of any one individual company.

Two alternatives were recommended by STAC – a 1,500-mile range Mach 1.2 aircraft and a 3,000-mile (transatlantic) machine that would fly faster, at Mach 1.8. Duncan Sandys, then Britain's Minister of Defence, responded with commissions to Bristol and Hawker Siddeley. The Bristol Type 198 proposal, which began as a Mach 1.3 'M-Wing' design, but was changed first to a slender 'delta' wing with overwing engines to fly at Mach 1.8, and then with underwing engines at Mach 2.2, resulted. It was to be powered by six developed Bristol Olympus turbojets. The 198 was abandoned in favour of a smaller four-engined version, the Type 223. Bristol was given the go ahead for the reduced weight BAC 223 study. Collaboration with other countries was built into the contract. It was at this time that Duncan Sandys forced the amalgamation of aircraft and aero-engine companies. The British Aircraft Corporation (BAC) was formed from Bristol Aircraft Ltd, Vickers Armstrong (Aircraft) and English Electric Aviation, while Bristol-Siddeley Engines Ltd (BSEL) was a grouping of Bristol Engines and Armstrong Siddeley. Sir George Edwards, who was to play a key part in the Concorde story, became Executive Director for aircraft of the new BAC.

Meanwhile, the nationalised French aircraft industry had grown rapidly after the end of the Second World War, its main success being the Sud Est Caravelle jet transport which used Rolls-Royce engines and the de Havilland Comet nose structure. After amalgamation with Sud Ouest (SNCASO) it became Sud Aviation and studied a supersonic Super Caravelle airliner design. At the June 1961 Paris Air Show, the French company displayed a model of the Super

Did you know?

The first passenger reservation for Concorde was taken in 1960, nine years before the first test flights.

3

Caravelle. Although it was not built, it was designed as a 2,000-mile range, 70-seat supersonic airliner.

Discussions took place between senior staff in Britain and France, including Sir Archibald Russell (technical director of Bristol Aircraft), but little common ground was reached. Meanwhile inter-governmental talks had proceeded satisfactorily. On 29 November 1962, an agreement for the joint design, development and manufacture of a 100-seat supersonic airliner was signed and registered at The Hague. It included clauses about each country having equal responsibility for the project, bearing equal shares of the cost, and sharing equally the proceeds of sales.

There were to be two integrated organisations taken from British and French firms: BAC and Sud Aviation for the airframe; Bristol Siddeley Engines and SNECMA for the engine. Julian Amery, as Minister of Aviation, was able to persuade both parties not to include a break clause because of the extremely high costs to which a remaining partner could be committed. This little known fact must have been substantially significant in later years in the turbulent history of Concorde's development.

"It is not unreasonable to look upon Concorde as a miracle. Who would have predicted that the combination of two governments, two airframe companies, two engine companies each with different cultures, languages and measurement would have produced a technical achievement the size of Concorde?"

Brian Trubshaw

Design and development of the revolutionary new airliner needed the solution of many complex technological problems, if the collaborating companies were to achieve their aim of manufacturing a safe and reliable supersonic transport (SST). The 'aerodynamic' shape of the wing was not only required to produce Mach 2 cruise efficiency, but also safe handling at low speed, to allow the SST to fit into standard airport approach patterns. The known change of trim at Mach 1 was to be compensated by automatic fuel transfer from trim tanks. There were problems to be faced from kinetic heating resulting from air friction which, during extended periods of supersonic flight, would raise the temperature of certain areas of the aircraft's structure to a figure where conventional light alloys would be unable to maintain their strength. This required the development of a new and improved aluminium alloy.

It was already known that air breathing jet engines would not work with the air entering them at Mach 2. Consequently the intakes were designed to incorporate computer controlled 'ramps' which, by restructuring the entry area, would generate controlled shock waves to slow the air from Mach 2 to Mach 0.5 in just 11 feet. The tail unit consisted only of a vertical fin and rudder, control in pitch and in roll was provided by six elevons spaced across the trailing-edge of the delta wing. The landing gear was of the hydraulically retractable tricycle type, with twin wheels on the nose unit and a four-wheel bogie on each main unit.

Much of Concorde's total fuel capacity was contained within the wing, but a percentage was held in four fuselage tanks.

Did you know?

Great Britain and France started working separately towards a supersonic aircraft in 1956. They were working along such similar lines that in 1962 they decided to develop one jointly.

The fuel was used for two other tasks in addition to fuelling the engines. Firstly, the large volume of fuel within the wing structure acted as a 'heat sink' to reduce the wing temperature in prolonged supersonic flight; and secondly, fuel was transferred automatically throughout the network of storage tanks to maintain the aircraft's centre of gravity (CG) while in the cruise. In addition, a group of trim tanks maintained the correct relationship between the aircraft's CG and its aerodynamic centre of pressure, fuel being moved aft during acceleration, and forward as the aircraft returned to subsonic flight. Like a praying mantis, the aircraft's high angle of attack as it approached to land required a 'droop nose' to give the pilot adequate forward visibility. Add to all the many engineering issues, the need for metric conversions, since the British (and US) aircraft industry was still using Imperial units of measurement, while the French (and the rest of Europe) were rooted in metric units workload there were also the language differences, political constraints and national pride.

"The joint French-British project to create a supersonic passenger service began as a dream in the late 1950s.
By 1962, they came up with a design and in 1969 it flew."

André Turcat

Design work proceeded on the Mach 2, transatlantic capable SST and the first metal was cut for test specimens in May 1963. It had been agreed that components would be built at only one place, but that assembly lines would be both at Filton and Toulouse. Design, development and construction was shared between Aérospatiale and BAC, with the French partner responsible for the wings and wing control surfaces; rear cabin section; air conditioning, hydraulics, navigation and radio systems; and flying controls. BAC was responsible for the three forward fuselage sections, rear fuselage; vertical tail surfaces; engine nacelles and ducting; engine installation, fire warning and extinguishing systems; electrical, fuel and oxygen systems; and noise and thermal insulation.

The development cost of the project in 1962 was estimated to be between £150m and £170m. Because of subsequent inflation, devaluation of the pound, reworking of the design in 1964 for just the long haul version – and the longer time it took to complete, the whole project eventually cost very much more. The cost share was also agreed with the UK being charged with 60 per cent of the engine and 40 per cent of the airframe.

From the start of the programme it was clear that the Bristol Olympus turbojet, already operational in the Avro Vulcan bomber, would be the selected powerplant. Bristol Aero-engines had privately developed the Olympus, despite government policy of 1957 that had decreed there would only be one large engine programme, centred on the Rolls-Royce Conway. Because of the foresight and wisdom of Sir Reginald Verdon-Smith, Chairman of the Bristol Aeroplane Co,

Did you know?
Proving the aerodynamic shape of Concorde took over 5,000 hours of subsonic, transonic and supersonic wing tunnel testing.

there would have been no engine immediately available, and suitable, for the SST. However, much development was required as the engine would have to operate in a higher temperature environment, at a higher turbine entry temperature and the engine components had to fit into a square nacelle. Furthermore, afterburners were needed for take-off and initial climb (the first, and only time, they have been fitted to engines on a civilian airliner), and also for acceleration through Mach 1.0 up to Mach 1.7. Thrust reversers were required to reduce the landing run after it touched down. These two items were the responsibility of the French engine manufacturer Société Nationale d'Etude et de Construction de Moteurs d'Aviation (SNECMA).

An interesting feature of the build programme was the use, for delivery of large components between the factories, of the Conroy Super Guppy freighter (a development of the Boeing Stratoliner), with its 25ft diameter upper fuselage. Two aircraft were acquired from Aero Spacelines in the USA and two more were modified in France using US kits.

"It stands for excellence, for Europe and for the Entente Cordiale."

Tony Benn, Bristol MP and Energy Minister when he tried to justify the final French 'E' that crept into Concorde's name

Moves to capture what was then considered to be a lucrative market were followed closely by interested parties in the USA and the USSR. In the USA, the Federal Aviation Administration (FAA) sponsored a competition for the design and development of a supersonic transport aircraft with intercontinental range. Boeing's Model 2707 was selected and the company was awarded a contract, on 1 May 1967, for the construction of two prototypes. It was envisaged as a 350-passenger aircraft that would have a normal cruising speed of Mach 2.7 and a range of 4,000 miles (6,440km) with 313 passengers. Good low-speed performance, for take-off, approach, and landing, would be ensured by the use of variable-geometry wings (swing wings). It was discovered, as the design progressed, that there were structural and weight problems from the proposed wings. This resulted in a re-design as the Model 2707-300, with fixed 'gull-wings'. President Richard Nixon gave the go-ahead for the production design of this version on 23 September 1969. The US spent nearly $1 billion on the Boeing 2707 before the development of an American SST came to an end on 24 March 1971, when the US Senate voted against providing the necessary finance for the construction of this aircraft. Politicians there, as in Britain and France, feared both the cost and the technical unknowns. They were also successfully intimidated by a powerful environmental lobby.

In the Soviet Union, design and development of an SST followed even more closely upon the moves in Britain and France, a model of the design proposals being exhibited at the Paris Air Show in 1965. The

Did you know?
Since they entered commercial service, British Airways' Concordes operated almost 50,000 flights, clocked up more than 140,000 flying hours, over 100,000 of them supersonically, and travelled some 140 million miles.

Tupolev Tu-144 had many features in common with Concorde and it was dubbed 'Concordski' by some western journalists who tried to establish that the Russians had spied on the Anglo-French project and stolen some of its key technical features. The Tu-144 made its maiden flight two months before Concorde 001 – and beat it, too, in reaching the magic figure of Mach 2 – twice the speed of sound. Although it was used for a short period by Aeroflot for cargo operations, the Tu-144 was not able to enter passenger-carrying commercial service.

"To decide not to venture in this field, while America and perhaps Russia and France go ahead, could well mean contracting out of the large passenger aircraft industry."

R.A. Butler, Deputy Prime Minister in November 1962.

Did you know?
Concorde's structure had to cope with temperatures as low as –45°C at subsonic speed and up to +140°C in supersonic flight.

The first Concorde prototype, 001, was rolled out at Toulouse on 11 December 1967, giving the world its first view outside of this beautiful aircraft. Much work remained and it was not until August 1968 that taxi trials took place. The event that everyone was waiting for, not least the employees of BAC and Aérospatiale, took place at Toulouse on 2 March 1969. André Turcat took the first prototype on its maiden flight, limited to 250kts and 10,000ft altitude, it was watched by millions of TV viewers, who saw it land 42 minutes later.

"Finally the big bird flies, and I can now say that it flies pretty well."

André Turcat, French Test Pilot, after 001's maiden flight

The first prototype Concorde was officially rolled out at Toulouse-Blagnac on 11 December 1967.

Did you know?
Concorde was the world's only supersonic passenger aircraft, cruising at more than twice the speed of sound at around 1,350mph, and at an altitude of up to 60,000ft (over 11 miles high). A typical New York crossing took a little less than three and a half hours. Travelling westwards, the five-hour time difference meant Concorde 'arrived before it had taken off', in local time at least. It flew faster than a speeding bullet.

Concorde 001 lifting off
on its historic maiden
flight at Toulouse on
2 March 1969 with
André Turcat at the
controls.

BAC's Chief Test Pilot Brian Trubshaw flew the second Concorde G-BSST from Filton on 9 April 1969 for the first time.

In Britain the great moment came at 2.24pm on 9 April 1969, when Concorde 002 G-BSST thundered along Filton's runway and soared gracefully into the air. 002 banked over the River Severn, its speed limited to 250kt and 10,000ft altitude and headed for Gloucestershire where it made its scheduled landing at the Flight Test Centre established at RAF Fairford. Here a crowd of 10,000 had assembled to see this historic first touchdown of a supersonic airliner in Britain. It was flown by the late Brian Trubshaw, the British Aircraft Corporation's Chief Test Pilot, who was responsible for Concorde's flight test programme and the base at Fairford, with its staff of 500.

Test flying proceeded and the two prototypes flew at the Paris Air Show at Le Bourget in June 1969. Concorde 001 first achieved Mach 1 on 1 October 1969 and, within another month, airline pilots first flew at

Did you know?

The characteristic droop nose was lowered to give the pilots' visibility for take-off and landing.

002 landing at RAF Fairford, the UK Concorde Flight Test Centre, after its maiden flight which was accompanied by a Canberra chase aircraft.

001 was joined at the airshow by 002/G-BSST flying from Fairford each day for a coordinated flying display.

Mach 1. 002 exceeded Mach 1 on 25 March 1970. The important stage of reaching Mach 2 was achieved with 001 on 4 November 1970 and with 002 just eight days later.

By June 1971, the two Concordes had reached 500 flying hours and 001 had made the first intercontinental flight – to Dakar, West Africa (2,500 miles in two hours and

Flying over Paris on 29 May 1969, Concorde 001/F-WTSS had its public debut at the Paris Air Show at Le Bourget.

During a two-week South American Tour in September 1971, the French prototype was photographed flying over Rio de Janeiro.

seven minutes). The prototypes were never intended to carry fare-paying passengers, but they proved that the supersonic transport was feasible and broke previously untested 'barriers'. 001 was used for a sales and demonstration tour which began on 4 September 1971. More or less simultane- ously, 002 was giving demonstration flights to interested airlines, politicians and the press. In June 1972, Concorde 002 began a 45,000 mile sales tour of 12 countries in the Far East and Australia. Early the following year, the same Concorde carried out hot and high airfield trials in South Africa. Perhaps one of the most significant flights was the first Concorde visit to the USA, with 002 flying in for the opening of Dallas Fort Worth Airport in September 1973. The return leg from Washington to Paris was in a record time of three hours 33 minutes.

"Everyone involved in the project had a great deal of pride in Concorde and still does. Concorde was conceived for engineers and developed by engineers. Certainly with a project of the complexity of Concorde, it could not be seen as anything other than a supreme team effort."

Sir Archibald Russell

Did you know?

The four specially modified Rolls-Royce/SNECMA Olympus 593 engines gave more than 38,000lb of thrust each. Reheat was added to the final stage of the engine to produce the extra power required for take-off and transition to supersonic flight. They were the most powerful pure jet engines fitted to an airliner in commercial service.

20

21

Ground-crew prepare G-BSST at Jan Smuts Airport, Johannesburg, South Africa in January 1973 for a 'hot and high' performance test flight.
(Rolls-Royce Bristol)

Some famous passengers

Prince Philip was the first member of the Royal Family to fly on Concorde in January 1972. The Queen flew five years later.

With British colours on one side and French on the other, F-WTSA visited Dallas-Fort Worth Airport, Texas in September 1973. (Arthur Gibson Collection)

F-WTSA, the second pre-production Concorde, at the Paris Air Show in June 1973 where it displayed and also made nine passenger demonstration flights. (PRM Aviation)

The first pre-production aircraft G-AXDN was rolled out at Filton on 20 September 1971. It had the 'new' nose/visor to give the pilots a better forward view.

The two pre-production Concordes, that incorporated a longer forward fuselage, more powerful engines, refined wing geometry and a revised glazed visor, were next off the lines. They first flew on 17 December 1971 (01 from Filton) and 10 January 1973 (02 with the production rear fuselage, from Toulouse).

Because of the complexity of the aircraft and its wide-ranging requirement, seven Concordes were allocated to cover the various aspects of testing. These consisted of the two original non-production standard prototypes – two pre-production models and the first three production aircraft. Only the last one of the seven eventually entered service, the first four being preserved in museums and the next two being used for some years on further development flying.

Initial flight testing from Fairford was devoted to proving the design concept and

The first pre-production aircraft G-AXDN under assembly in the Brabazon Hangar at Filton in 1969.

establishing the performance characteristics of the airframe, engines and systems as one complete unit, throughout the full flight envelope. This progressed to certification flying to prove the aircraft safe in normal commercial operation, including a programme of route proving to demonstrate the

01/G-AXDN getting airborne for a test flight in 1973 after it had been up-graded nearer to the production standard, including a new digital intake control system.
(Rolls-Royce Bristol)

Did you know?

Concorde was subjected to 5,000 hours of testing by the time it was certified for passenger flight, making it the most tested aircraft in aviation history.

capability of normal airline operation with passengers.

The first four aircraft were purely test flying laboratories, each one carrying up to 12 tons of specially developed test instrumentation. The pre-production aircraft, with their lengthened fuselages, were able to seat up to 139 passengers at a 34in seat pitch. Because of the sonic boom problem, much of the test flying from Fairford had to be done over the sea, either over the Bay of Biscay or the North Sea. For some supersonic performance measuring, an 800-mile straight route was established along a north-south line running over the coasts of Western Scotland, Wales and Cornwall. At an early stage in the development programme, overseas flights were made, to sell the concept of the aircraft and gain acceptance in likely areas of operation.

"There was intense world-wide interest and personalities from Prince Philip downward wanted to see what made Concorde tick. I found myself flying around the world to promote the aeroplane. Landing at Bombay the whole staff lined the runway. It was like trying to land on a football pitch."

Brian Trubshaw.

▲
Photographed at the Filton Families Day event in 1974, Concorde 01/G-AXDN made one of the fastest 'civil' crossings of the North Atlantic later that year.
(Rolls-Royce Bristol)

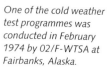

Despite the inherent problems of Concorde, posed by the fact that it was an SST, and including such items as engine noise, sonic boom, fuel consumption and cost, there was initially considerable interest in the aircraft and its earth-shrinking potential for business and VIP travel. A significant number of the world's airlines including Air Canada, Air France, American Airlines, BOAC, Eastern Air Lines, Japan Air Lines, Lufthansa, Pan American, QANTAS, Sabena, TWA and United Air Lines were all seriously looking at ordering Concorde. Potential sales of more than 70 aircraft were on the cards and the prospects for a commercial success then seemed quite within the bounds of possibility. Unfortunately this did not materialise for many reasons, not least the high cost of purchasing and operating the SST at a time of world-wide economic decline. On 19 July 1974 the two governments announced that Concorde production would be limited to 16 aircraft. Of these the first two #201/F-WTSB and #202/G-BBDG would be used for trials and further development work; BOAC/British Airways and Air France would each take delivery of five aircraft and the final four would be

Runway undulation tests were carried out by Concorde 202/G–BBDG, shown here at Singapore in 1974.

The first British
production Concorde
(202/G-BBDG) taking-
off from Fairford in July
1974.

available to purchase by another airline or airlines.

The first production Concorde (201) flew from Toulouse on 6 December 1973 and, on its 160 minute maiden flight, reached Mach 1.57. The first UK-built production Concorde (202) flew on 13 February 1974 and also went supersonic on this first flight. These were followed in 1975 by four aircraft, two in France and two in the UK, with the same

number getting airborne in 1976. The last two 'ordered' Concordes were flown in 1977.

Extensive test flying and route proving continued with the programme towards certification. A special category Certificate of Airworthiness (CofA) was issued to Concorde 204 (G-BOAC) on 30 June 1975, for route-proving trials, with the Olympus 593 engines receiving their type certification on 29 September 1975. This was after a flight test

Concordes 204/G-BOAC (painted), 206/G-BOAA and 208/G-BOAB under construction at Filton in 1974.

programme that had taken six and a half years. All the British testing had been done from Fairford involving ten aircraft that made some 2,480 flights with 5,540 hours in the air. Total development cost, shared between the two countries, was £1,130 million, none of which was recovered from sales. The final section of the flight test and certification programme was undertaken by Concorde 204 – G-BOAC, which included flying around 1,000 hours of route proving. When the full British CofA was granted on 5 December 1975, the way was now clear for Concorde to enter service.

"While the US aimed for the moon, Britain aimed for
supersonic flight – and we made it, too."

Reginald Turnhill, former BBC Aerospace and Defence Correspondent

◀
The second Concorde handed over to BA, G-BOAC briefly returned to Filton in mid-1976.

◀◀
With a Certificate of Airworthiness granted by the UK CAA, G-BOAC started endurance flights including this one to Bahrain on 7 July 1975.

▶▶
British Concorde prototype G-BSST was retired to the FAA Museum at RNAS Yeovilton on 4 March 1976 and is on display in the Concorde Hall.
(PRM Aviation)

On 21 January 1976, in a carefully choreographed count down in front of the world's press and TV, British Airways Concorde 206 (G-BOAA) opened up for take-off from Heathrow to fly to Bahrain, at the same time as Air France 205 (F-BVFA) left Paris for Rio de Janeiro, via Dakar. The British Airways flight was subsonic as far as Venice, but reached Mach 2 over the Adriatic Sea and across the Middle East. Air

First flown on 3 March 1974 Concorde 206/ G-BOAA was the first aircraft delivered to British Airways on 14 January 1976.
(Rolls-Royce Bristol)

Did you know?

The commercial supersonic era commenced on 21 January 1976, with British Airways flying from London Heathrow to Bahrain and Air France from Paris to Rio de Janeiro.

France was able to fly supersonic from the Bay of Biscay and south to Dakar.

Shortly after, the US Secretary of Transportation, William T. Coleman Jr finally gave approval for British Airways and Air France to operate into New York and Washington for a 16-month period. Concorde had already flown into Dallas, Boston, Miami, Los Angeles and San Francisco on demonstration flights.

The Washington service was opened from London and Paris on 24 May 1976. On this occasion, British Airways planned to land its Concorde (204) at Washington just ahead of the Air France Concorde, finishing in a nose-to-nose pose in front of the tall control tower. Both Concordes performed perfectly, as they had done four months earlier at the start of their commercial careers.

Flights continued with an average load factor of 80 per cent and it appeared that New York was being bypassed. New York flights had to be cleared with the Port Authority, who made it impossible by a ban on noise grounds. Despite a detailed analysis by the manufacturers on flight techniques, which was presented to the Port, it maintained its stance. It became increasingly apparent that there would have to be a legal battle before Concorde could gain landing rights at New York. It was not until October 1977 that a US Supreme Court ruled against the ban, and the airlines immediately announced that proving flights would arrive two days later. Protesters and full noise measurement gear was gathered there on 19 October 1977 as Concorde 201 (F-WTSB) landed. Over 500 members of the press assembled in a hangar for crew interviews. Next day, Captain Brian Walpole, BA Flight Technical Manager, took off at full power,

afterburners on, following a Boeing 707 and Boeing 747. Next day the tests were repeated – the opposition collapsed.

Brian Walpole was again on board for the first regular airline service to New York on 22 November 1977 – this time with the Air France Concorde landing ahead, but they taxied in to meet nose-to-nose on the taxiway.

The British Airways route to Bahrain was extended to Singapore in conjunction with

Air France Concorde F-BTSC was given temporary markings for a role in the movie *Airport 79 The Concorde*.
(Via Air France)

Singapore Airlines in December 1977 and continued until November 1980, with interruptions caused by the Malaysian Government withdrawing overflying rights. With the withdrawal of supersonic overflying permission the Concorde route to Singapore had to go south of Sri Lanka (Ceylon), adding some 200 miles. Also the Malaysian Government subsequently withdrew flying rights over the Straits of Malacca. This service was abandoned when the ensuing world recession brought about a drop in Concorde's load totals between London and Singapore.

A similar agreement with Braniff Airlines took the Washington service through to Dallas from early 1979 until mid-1980. For this service the Concordes were given 'hybrid' British and American registrations. G-BOAA, for example, became G-N94AA.

"One must sample it to believe it, for here I sit in a comfortable cabin in the calm air nearly 60,000ft up, hurtling along faster than the speed of a cannon shell, eating caviar and drinking exquisite champagne that rests without a ripple on my table. This is history."

Air Cdre E M Donaldson, *Daily Telegraph* air correspondent reporting on Concorde's first service to Bahrain

G-BOAD/N-94AD had Singapore Airlines markings painted on its port side in 1980 when a joint Concorde service was operated for a few months.

Concorde had been expected to be the first in a line of supersonic transports, but the early demise of the Russian Tu-144 and America's Boeing 2707 left it in a unique position. The Anglo-French SST, while advanced in terms of speed – flying from London to New York in three-hours – was relatively small and marginal in range for successful commercial operations world-wide. Although, when it entered service it was not much noisier than some of the contemporary jet airliners, within a decade a new generation of much quieter and very much more efficient turbofan engines was powering new, large, wide-body airliners.

The 'cost' of getting Concorde to cruise at Mach 2 was high. The Olympus engines were not only noisy but very thirsty. Fuel crises across the decades served to put up the cost of operating the airliner and played into the hands of the environmental lobby. Then there was the supersonic 'boom'. As an aircraft passes Mach 1 it creates a shock wave that reaches the ground as a loud double 'boom'. Governments around the world banned Concorde from exceeding the speed of sound over their land. This meant that the airlines flying the airliner had to route Concorde over water, or sparsely populated areas, when it was travelling 'faster than sound' and decelerate to subsonic speed over land. Of course this negated the value of flying in Concorde if its speed was reduced to the same as other airliners. These environmental factors were seized upon by the 'anti-Concorde brigade', particularly in the USA, where political support gave them added weight. Cancellation of the Boeing SST programme made many US politicians sensitive to any success that the European airliner might have at the apparent expense of the US aircraft industry.

Did you know?
Due to Concorde's high cruise altitude (50,000-60,000ft) and the aerodynamic properties of its delta wing, its passengers experienced only one sixth of the turbulence experienced by subsonic jet travellers.

"A dream of supersonic flight must have been in the minds of all the great pioneers of
aviation from the Wright brothers onwards and predictably it first came to reality in
military aircraft. But Concorde was different because it was born without any military
application and it was seen as a way of shrinking the world to bring people together,
if they could afford to pay the fare, of course."

Tony Benn, MP and former Government Minister

The last four production Concordes were 'sold' to Air France and British Airways in the absence of any other customers. The final Concorde to be completed was #216/G-BFKX later G-BOAF, that was flown from Filton on 20 April 1979. A total of 20 Concordes was built: two prototypes, two pre-production and 16 production. Air France operated a maximum of six Concordes, having retired one of its first five in 1982, whereas British Airways operated all seven UK-built Concordes.

On 1 May 1982 British Airways' Concorde Division was formed, at the same time as the UK Government handed over Concorde operations to the then State-owned BA, writing off the development costs. By 21 January 1986, ten years after the SST's entry into service, Concorde had already amassed 71,000 supersonic flying hours.

Initially there were seven flights per week on the London–New York route and these were then increased to ten and subsequently to 14 (two per day). The Washington route ceased in 1994 because most passengers wanted New York and not Washington. In

Concorde 216, the last Filton-built aircraft and unsold at the time, made its first flight on 27 January 1978.

49

➤
Concorde 216 here flying in stormy weather in August 1985, was sold to BA for a nominal sum and re-registered G-BOAF.
(PRM Aviation)

➤➤
BA Concorde G-BOAC was the first to fly with the new 'British' livery.

the late 1980s charter services were introduced to Barbados which subsequently became a scheduled service, although mainly in the winter months. Charter flights, which always made a profit, expanded and sometimes equated to 10 per cent of the whole operation. Air France continued using five Concordes following similar patterns of operations as British Airways. The reliability of Concorde was very important as the subsonic alternative in the event of a delay was not what the customer had paid for. Consequently, a standby Concorde was available at Heathrow every morning. By the summer of 2000 Concorde had flown to 250 different destinations throughout the world.

"It's hard to believe there will never be another supersonic aeroplane – inspired by Concorde's achievements."

Brian Trubshaw

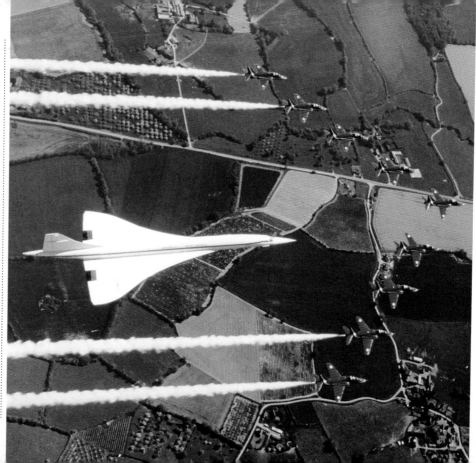

 When Concorde G-BBDG flew with the Red Arrows in 1983 the RAF team had re-equipped with Hawks.
(Arthur Gibson Collection)

➤➤ Concorde G-BOAG returned to service in 1985 after an extensive refit and was painted in the new BA 'Landor' livery.
(British Airways)

◄
Ready for take-off. G-BOAA lined-up for departure from Runway 28L at London-Heathrow in February 1986.
(Allan Burney)

◄◄
Arthur Gibson's classic photograph of Concorde G-BOAG flying with the Red Arrows Hawks over the QE2 in 1985.
(Arthur Gibson Collection)

Two Concordes G-BOAC and 'AD in the BA maintenance hangar at Heathrow in March 1986.
(Allan Burney)

The white paint scheme on BA Concordes stands out against this stormy sky at an airshow in 1986.
(PRM Aviation)

➤ *G-BOAD flying past the stored Concorde G-BBDG at Filton Families Day on 27 June 1987.*

➤➤ *A record-breaking flight was made by G-BOAA from New York to London-Heathrow in two hours 55 minutes and 15 seconds on 7 February 1988.*
(PRM Aviation)

With its nose drooped
12½° and the aircraft
pitched up 11° Concorde
G-BOAA touches down
on a charter flight to
RNAS Yeovilton.
(PRM Aviation)

▶▶

A British Airways
Concorde and the RAF
Red Arrows make a
spectacular flypast at the
International Air Tattoo at
Fairford in 1989.
(PRM Aviation)

> Air France's F-BVFF, the last Toulouse-built Concorde, made a charter flight to the RAF airshow at Finningley, Yorks.
(Andrew March)

Did you know?

More than 2.5 million passengers flew supersonically on British Airways flights since the aircraft went into service in 1976.

Concorde G-BOAC lined up for take-off with supersonic charter flight passengers at Fairford in July 1994.
(PRM Aviation)

Some famous passengers

Phil Collins took Concorde from London to New York to appear on both sides of the Atlantic in one day for the Live Aid music event in aid of famine relief in Africa.

Returning to the former Concorde test base at Fairford, G-BOAB flew in to the 1996 Royal International Air Tattoo with a full load of passengers.
(Andrew March)

▶▶

The most surprising paint scheme was carried by F-BTSD for two weeks in April 1996 while promoting a new Pepsi Cola image.

➤
*G-BOAF was the first
of the BA fleet to receive
the £1 million internal
makeover and be painted
with the Chatham
Historic Dockyard
tail flag.*
(British Airways)

Did you know?
It measures 204 feet in length but that stretched between 6 and 10 inches in flight, due to the heating of the airframe which also ensured the airframe was effectively corrosion-free.

It was the turn of
Concorde G-BOAE to fly
into the 1998 Royal
International Air Tattoo.
(PRM Aviation)

Did you know?

There were more US
Astronauts than BA
Concorde pilots.

A unique quartet of Concordes flying together in 1999 to mark the 30th anniversary of the airline's formation.
(British Airways)

Did you know?
On the North Atlantic route, the Concorde passenger, having completed the meal, would be descending to the destination, whilst the subsonic counterpart would be facing another 3½ hours.

Concorde's brilliant 32-year safety record was shattered on 25 July 2000 when Air France F-BTSC, on a non-scheduled operation, crashed on take-off at Paris Charles de Gaulle Airport, killing all 109 people on board and four on the ground. The unimaginable had happened. Air France immediately grounded its Concorde fleet and British Airways followed as soon as the likely cause had been identified. After careful study by Accident Investigators it was concluded that the accident had been caused when the Concorde struck a piece of metal that had apparently fallen off a preceding DC-10. This ruptured a tyre that disintegrated, throwing large pieces of rubber against the underside of Concorde's wing, which in turn caused a fuel tank to rupture. The escaping fuel was ignited by the nearest engine that was at full power with reheat.

The question was soon being asked whether Concorde should fly again. British Airways announced that it was determined to put the airliner back into service, provided it could be done safely and with the complete confidence of all concerned. All modifications were completed by mid-2001 and during this time the interiors of all BA Concordes were redesigned with new seats, interior decor, galleys and toilets as part of a £14 million programme of investment, announced in January 2000, to ensure the interior of the aircraft was as elegant as the exterior. *Conran & Partners*, led by Sir Terence Conran, advised on colours, fabrics and accessories, working with London-based design consultancy, *Factory Design* and *Britax Aircraft Interior Systems* of Camberley, Surrey. Features of the interior design included: new seats with ink-blue Connolly leather and fabric with a cradle

After the tragic accident in July 2000, Air France's F-BVFC was stranded in New York and was not flown back to Paris until 21 September.
(AIRTime Publishing Inc)

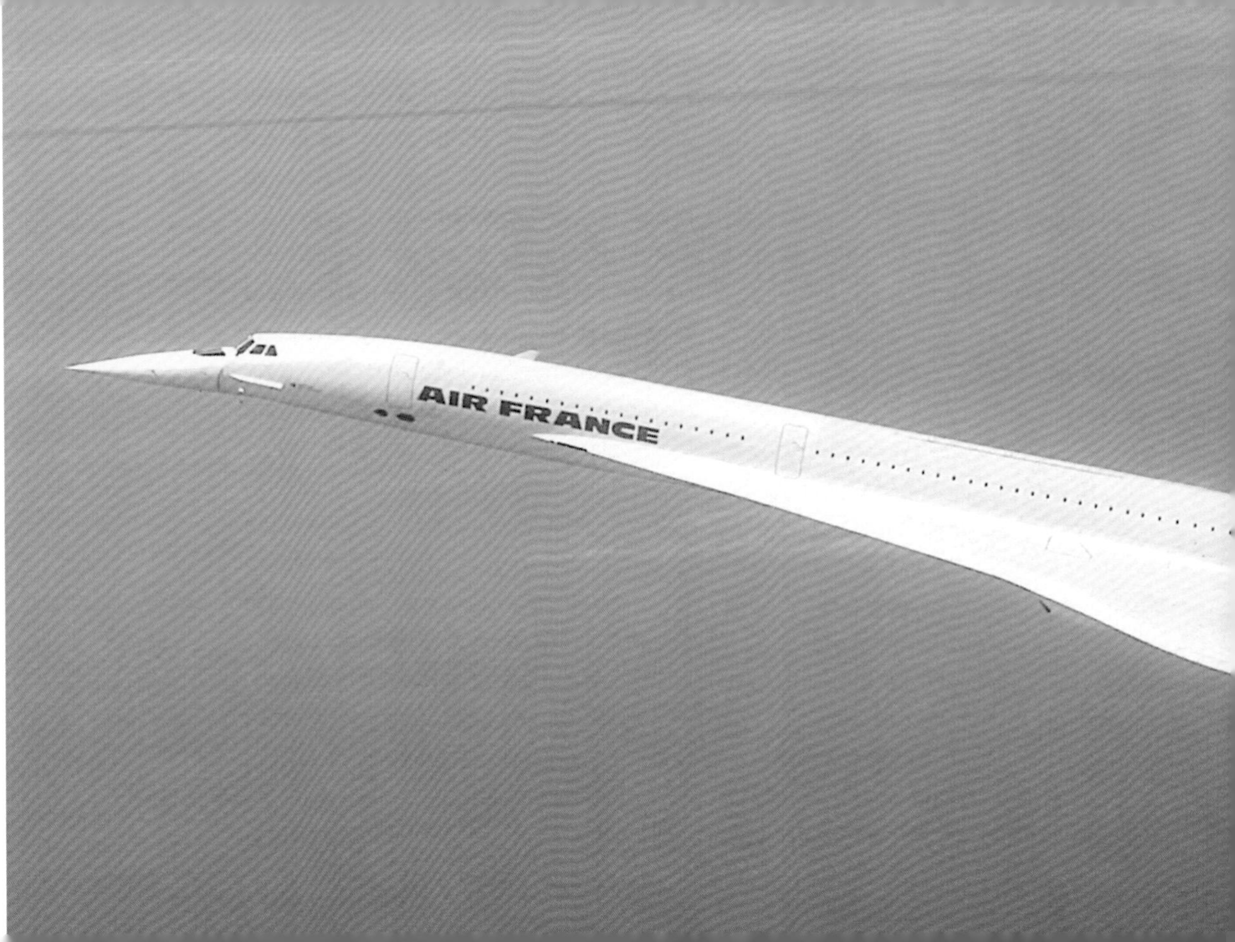
AIR FRANCE

mechanism, footrest and contoured head rest for more comfort and support. The design used new technology and materials that were 20 per cent lighter in weight which led to a saving of almost £1 million a year in fuel efficiencies. The cabin had a much lighter and brighter interior with different lighting filters that gave a fresher look. The menus on Concorde were refreshed and revived prior to its relaunch in 2002. Customers could expect dishes such as smoked salmon fish cakes, with Bloody Mary relish and shrimp risotto, breast of guinea fowl with lemon, thyme and baby vegetables or lobster truffle salad with crisp french beans. Concorde had its own cellar containing some of the finest vintage wines available that were changed every month. Champagne on-board included Dom Perignon and Krug. White wines included Puilgny-Montrachet 1er Cru and

◀
The second Air France Concorde to fly again, F-BTSD was airborne on 11 April 2001, making a three-hour supersonic flight.
(Air France)

Chablis Grand Cru. Those who preferred red could choose from some of the finest clarets and burgundies, including Château Pichon Comtesse Lalande and Les Forts de Latour.

On 16 July 2001 G-BOAF took-off from Heathrow on a full supersonic verification flight and a series of operational assessment flights was made over the following weeks. The Certificate of Airworthiness was restored on 6 September 2001 – the dream could begin once more. With everything running favourably for the reintroduction of Concorde scheduled services in early November, British Airways commenced ticket sales on 16 October.

Air France achieved similar progress with its four Concordes, and the two airlines operated their fare-paying passenger services on 7 November 2001. The weekly British Airways service to Barbados was resumed on 1 December 2001, when the first of 21 return flights was made to the island. The demand for this service was consistently up to expectations and initially the British Airways load factors on the 'bread and butter' weekday route to New York was regularly over 70 per cent.

Five BA Concordes (G-BOAC, G-BOAD, G-BOAE. G-BOAF and G-BOAG) were eventually modified and their CofAs restored. The sixth (G-BOAB) was scheduled to have its modification programme started in mid-2003, while the seventh aircraft G-BOAA was kept as a source of spares at Heathrow. Four Air France aircraft were modified and returned to service (F-BVFA, F-BVFB, F-BVFC and F-BTSD). With the two airlines celebrating the 25th anniversary of their scheduled Concorde services to New York on 22 November, all seemed well.

◄

BA Concorde G-BOAF was the first of the fleet to fly again, leaving Heathrow for a verification flight on 17 July 2001.
(British Airways)

F-BTSD became the first
of the Air France
Concordes to return to
service, flying to New York
on 7 November 2001.
(Air France)

"I feel safer on Concorde than I do
driving on the M3. It's a huge, gas-
guzzling machine and yet it's beautiful."

Gordon Sumner, better known as Sting

MACH FEET
2.00 55500

The popular cabin machmeter showing the aircraft was flying at twice the speed of sound at 55,500ft during a charter flight.

Air France retired F-BTSD to the Musée de l'Air at Le Bourget where it arrived during the Paris Air Show on 14 June 2003.
(PRM Aviation)

Early in 2003 it became increasingly clear that everything was not going to plan with Concorde operations. After several weeks of rumours and denials, British Airways and Air France both suddenly announced on 10 April 2003 that they would make their last Concorde flight by the end of October. This untimely end to supersonic travel would come nearly 30 years after it began and with no replacement 'anywhere in sight'.

What had caused this sudden volte-face? A great deal of money had just been spent on upgrading and re-certificating Concorde following the Paris tragedy. The aircraft was cleared to fly until 2009 and this could have been extended to 2015. British Airways, in particular, was becoming increasingly optimistic about the airliner regaining its popularity across the Atlantic and its overall commercial viability.

The official reasons initially given were the world-wide downturn that had affected the airline business following the events of 11 September. British Airways' First and Business Class travel fell by over a quarter, which had severely constrained Concorde bookings. Air France had seen a more dramatic drop in

Operating BA Flight 001 to New York, G-BOAC climbs out of London-Heathrow on 24 August 2003.
(Richard Cooper)

numbers, and the airline suspected that it had also become a victim of some Americans boycotting the airline over France's stance at the UN on the war in Iraq.

Following the 10 April joint announcement Air France revealed that it was going to suspend scheduled services within a few weeks, on 31 May 2003, and completely retire its fleet no later than 1 November. British Airways reaffirmed that it would maintain its operation to the end of October and stop all Concorde flying during the following month. The die was cast – but how had this come about, the press was asking?

It appears that Air France's lack of enthusiasm for continued Concorde operations triggered support from Airbus, the successor to Aérospatiale, and British Aerospace, as design authority for the airliner. If Airbus withdrew its support for Concorde, neither

Did you know?

Concorde took-off at 220 kt, compared with 165 kt for most subsonic aircraft. Landing speeds were also higher. In other respects it performed in much the same way.

Concorde G-BOAC landing at London-Heathrow on 30 August 2003 after the last of the summer programme of Barbados flights. (Peter Cooper/Falcon Aviation Photos)

airline would be able to continue flying the airliner for scheduled, charter or special operations. The future of Concorde demanded that all three 'partners' should maintain the *status quo*.

Was there any political pressure behind the decision? The French government, majority shareholder in Air France, said it would respect the decision of the airline management on the supersonic airliners' future. "Any decision which Air France made would be accepted by the current shareholder", the French Secretary of State for Transport said. British Airways also confirmed that there had been no government intervention in the decision. "This abrupt end", a spokesman for the airline said, "had been made for commercial reasons alone, mainly due to falling premium passenger loads, which would no longer be able to fund upcoming costs".

A poignant shot of
G-BOAG heading off
into the sunset en route
to New York on
16 September 2003.
(Richard Cooper)

The airlines' plans to dispose of their Concorde fleets to museums across the world underlined the fact that there was no intention of selling them to any other operator. British Airways said firmly that its seven Concordes were 'not for sale' since Airbus, the successor to the joint Anglo-French manufacturers, would not allow any other airline than British Airways or Air France, to operate the prestigious plane.

Air France confirmed that Airbus had put the facts on the table and that the airline's decision had been taken 'in conjunction with the manufacturer'. Furthermore, even British Airways' suggestion that one of its fleet should be kept airworthy for appearances at airshows and special fly-pasts for another five to ten years was also rejected by the 'design authority', Airbus. Without the company's commitment to technical support the Civil Aviation Authority would not grant the necessary 'Permit to Fly' on these non-passenger carrying sorties.

"I believe that every effort should be made to keep Concorde flying as it is such an important symbol of British innovation."

Sir Richard Branson

G-BOAC embarking passengers for BA's goodbye to Concorde flight to Birmingham on 21 October.
(Richard Cooper)

Sunset for the Concorde
came at the end of
October 2003.
(Richard Cooper)

Did you know?

Concorde flew faster
than the Earth rotates.

G-BOAG receiving a
water salute at Heathrow
after Concorde's last ever
commercial flight, BA002
from New York, on
24 October 2003.
(Richard Cooper)

Air France accelerated its withdrawal, making the last commercial Concorde service from New York to Paris Charles de Gaulle Airport on 31 May 2003. On 28 May Air France announced that it was donating four of its Concordes to museums in France, Germany and the USA, while retaining the fifth (F-BVFF), that made its last flight on 11 June 2000, to be displayed at Charles de Gaulle Airport, Paris. Through the following month, they were ferried to their 'retirement' locations.

British Airways scheduled Concorde services to New York continued through the summer of 2003 and the weekend flights to Barbados ran from 26 July, ending on 30 August. BA organised a farewell tour of the UK and North America, visiting Birmingham, Belfast, Manchester, Cardiff and Edinburgh in the UK and Boston, Washington and Toronto across the Atlantic. British Airways'

Concorde operations ended in style on Friday 24 October 2003, when the last aircraft with paying passengers landed at London Airport just after 4 p.m. It was 'escorted' by two other Concorde special flights, the airliners landing within minutes of each other.

At 5.05 p.m. the era of supersonic passenger transport came officially to an end, when G-BOAG, with Captain Mike Bannister flying this final BA002 service from New York, touched down on Heathrow's runway 27 Right. *Alpha Golf* had entered British airspace for the last time at 4.15 p.m., dropping below the speed of sound off the west coast of Ireland.

> "Concorde will never really stop
> flying because it will live on
> in people's imagination."
> Air France Chairman Jean-Cyril Spinetta

The last ever Concorde flight by G-BOAF from London-Heathrow to Filton on 26 November 2003 included a flypast over Bristol and the Clifton Suspension Bridge.

➤
The last Concorde to be assembled at Filton, 216/G-BOAF made a final flypast over the airfield before landing.

Returning 'home', Concorde G-BOAF making the supersonic airliner's last touchdown at Filton on 26 November 2003.

Did you know?

Each British Airways Concorde when they were retired was young in terms of 'aeroplane years', having completed about the same number of take-offs and landings as a three-to-four year-old Boeing 737.

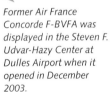

Former Air France Concorde F-BVFA was displayed in the Steven F. Udvar-Hazy Center at Dulles Airport when it opened in December 2003.

G-BOAD was loaded onto a barge for its final journey to the Intrepid Air & Space Museum, New York in November 2003.

Here dismantled at Filton, the first British production Concorde G-BBDG was taken by road to the Brooklands Museum at Weybridge in May 2004.
(PRM Aviation)

◀◀

Concorde G-BOAA passing the Houses of Parliament on a barge in April 2004 while en route to the Scottish Museum of Flight at East Fortune.
(Peter Cooper/Falcon Aviation Photos)

 The flight deck of
G-BOAF is illuminated
for visitors who also hear
a recording of the air
traffic controller and pilot
during its final flight into
Filton.
(PRM Aviation)

 Concorde G-BOAF is
preserved by Airbus UK
and the Bristol Aero
Collection at Filton.
(PRM Aviation)

101

Did you know?

About one in five of business people who were on the daily 10.30 a.m. flight from London to New York were home in the UK on the same day.

G-BOAF was the first Concorde to have the £1 million makeover of the interior, including new leather seats seen here in the rear cabin.
(PRM Aviation)

Visitors to Concorde can see the washroom/toilet at the front and rear of the aircraft.
(PRM Aviation)

◀

Concorde G-BOAC is preserved at the Manchester Airport Visitor Centre where it is open to the public.
(Gordon Bartley)

◀◀

'The Flight Engineer's Hat' trapped for posterity between panels when the airliner cooled following its last supersonic flight and landing at Filton.
(PRM Aviation)

Some famous passengers

Other supersonic celebrities included the late Diana, Princess of Wales, the Duchess of York, the late Queen Mother, Joan Collins, Sir Cliff Richard, Sir David Frost, Sir Elton John, Lady Margaret Thatcher, Tony Blair, Annie Lennox, Robert Redford, Sting, Sam Torrance, Kate Moss, Jodie Kidd, the late George Harrison and Ewan McGregor.

Flight Certificate

By travelling on
British Airways Concorde

G-BOAA on 28 August 1984 from New York to London

PETER R. MARCH

has joined the select group who have travelled at Mach II in the world's first supersonic passenger aircraft

Capt. B.Walpole General Manager Concorde

Capt D.Leney - BA9092

Concorde

Concorde

Many Concorde passengers have cherished the Flight Certificate detailing their supersonic journey given to them by the airline.

With 60 serious bids for one of the retired airliners, BA chose to send three of the Concordes to the USA and Barbados and keep four in the UK. Perhaps the most significant of these was the return of the last Concorde (216/G-BOAF) to Filton where it was first flown in April 1979, for preservation by Airbus UK and the Bristol Aero Collection, until it can be housed in the proposed new Bristol Heritage Museum. Just before 1 p.m. on Thursday 26 November 2003 Concorde G-BOAF touched down at Filton, bringing an end to the era of supersonic passenger flying. It is ironic that this occurred just 21 days before the world celebrated the 100th anniversary of the Wright Brothers first powered flight at Kitty Hawk, North Carolina on 17 December.

So at the end of the story there are 18 Concordes preserved in memory of the all too short supersonic passenger airliner age. These aircraft will serve as a lasting reminder of the unrivalled expertise and cutting edge technology in Britain and France, that produced the world's only successful supersonic airliner over four decades ago.

How can one sum up Concorde? Russia managed to fly its Tupolev Tu-144 before Concorde, but it never saw passenger service. The US aviation industry pinned its hopes on a Mach 3 project, but it never reached fruition. Meanwhile the Concorde fleet of British Airways and Air France reputedly flew more supersonic hours than all of the world's air forces have accumulated in the same period – and we called it Concorde when we glanced skyward, not a Concorde.

Concorde probably generated more pride, and more noise and environmental controversy, than any other civil airliner ever built. To whichever of these groups an indi-

Concorde on the big and small screens

Concorde appeared in many films and tv programmes over the years. These included: *Xanadu, Doctor Who, Airport '80: The Concorde, Live and Let Die, Coming to America, Johnny English, Long Good Friday, Record Breakers, Only Fools and Horses – Christmas edition 2001, Snatch, The Wild Geese, Absolutely Fabulous.*

vidual belonged, there are few who will not agree that Concorde, one of the first fruits of international collaboration, did prove a supreme technological success. It was an aircraft that everyone recognised, a noise that turned heads. There were few sights in the aviation world that created such an effect as to stop people in their tracks and look to the skies. Concorde was indeed in a class of its own.

"For guys like me who were ten years old or so when they first saw the pristine white needle streak across the sky, first heard the tremendously powerful engine roar, it will be the end of an era in aviation, the end of a dream and the realisation that, with every passing day, many such dreams fade into dim, if not cherished, memories."

Peter Combs

APPENDIX I – SPECIFICATION

Range: 4,300 miles (6,880km)

Engines: Four Rolls-Royce/SNECMA Olympus 593s, each producing 38,050lb thrust with 17% reheat

Take-off speed: 220 kt (250mph/400km/h)

Cruising speed: 1,350mph (2,150km/h/Mach 2) at 60,000ft

Landing speed: 187mph (300 km/h)

Length: 203ft 9in (62.1m)

Wingspan: 83ft 10in (25.56m)

Overall height: 37ft 1in (11.32m)

Fuselage width: 9ft 6in (2.9m)

Fuel capacity: 26,286 Imperial gallons (119,500 litres/95,600kg)

Fuel consumption: 5,638 Imperial gallons (25,629 litres/20,500kg) per hour

Maximum take-off weight: 408,000lb (185,060kg)

Maximum landing weight: 245,000lb (111,130 kg)

Payload (typical): 25,000lb (11,340kg)

Flight crew: Two pilots, one flight engineer

Cabin crew: Six

Accommodation Single Class: 108 passengers (38in pitch)

Hold space: 697 cu ft at 10lb/cu ft

Concorde statistics

Number of aircraft built:	20
Number of production aircraft:	16
Number of Concordes in service:	14
Fastest Atlantic crossing east to west	3 hr 6 min
Fastest Atlantic crossing west to east	2 hr 53 min
Number of production engines built:	88
Entered airline service:	1976
Total engine flying hours:	954,752
Total supersonic flying hours:	716,000
Total supersonic engine miles:	1 billion
Number of flights made by BA with Concorde	50,000 approx
Concord flew round the world (28, 238 miles in:	29 hr 59 min
Finally retired from airline service:	2003

APPENDIX II – CONCORDE MILESTONES

1956 Start of supersonic airline research in Europe.

1956 Supersonic Transport Aircraft Committee (STAC) established to study SST.

1959 STAC recommended design studies for separate Mach 1.2 and Mach 2 projects.

1960 British Airways' forerunner BOAC accepted its first Concorde reservation.

1961 Anglo-French discussions on commonality of SST requirements and design studies lead to investigation of possible collaboration. Discussions take place between BAC and Sud Aviation in Paris and at Weybridge.

1962 November: British and French governments signed agreement for joint design, development and manufacture of a supersonic airliner.

1963 First metal cut for test specimens.

1963 General de Gaulle made the first use of the Concorde name.

1963 Pan American, BOAC and Air France sign Concorde 'options'. Medium-range version enlarged.

1963 Labour Government announces it will review programme.

1963 US President John F. Kennedy backed the development of US SST.

1964 Announcement of developed aircraft with increased wing area and lengthened fuselage, providing accommodation of up to 118 passengers. Design subsequently 'frozen ' for prototype manufacture.

1964 July: Olympus 593 'D' (Derivative) engine first run at Filton.

1965 April: First metal cut for Concorde prototypes.

1965 May: Pre-production Concorde design (130 seats) announced.

1965 October: Prototype Concorde sub-assemblies started.

1965 November: Olympus 593 'B' (Big) engine first run at Filton.

1965 Government announces review complete, programme to continue despite financial and economic doubts.

1966 March: Sixteen ton centre fuselage/wing section for static and thermal testing delivered to CEAT, Toulouse.

1966 April: Final assembly of prototype 001 began at Toulouse.

1966 June: Concorde main flight simulator commissioned at Toulouse.

1966 June: Complete Olympus 593 engine and variable geometry exhaust testbed run at Melun-Villaroche, France.

1966 August: Final assembly of prototype 002 began at Filton.

1966 September: Avro Vulcan flying testbed with Olympus 593 made first flight. Olympus 593 first ran in Cell 3 high-altitude facility, NGTE Pyestock, England.

1966 Seventy foot-long fuselage and nose section delivered to RAE Farnborough for fatigue testing.

1967 Full-scale Concorde interior mock-up at Filton first presented to customer airlines.

1967 11 December: Roll-out of first prototype 001 at Toulouse.

1967 Options to purchase reached a total of 74 from 16 airlines.

1968 February: UK government announced £125m loan to launch production of aircraft and engines.

1968 September: Roll-out of second prototype 002 at Filton.

1969 2 March: Maiden flight of Concorde 001 from Toulouse.

1969 9 April: Maiden flight of Concorde 002 from Filton, Bristol landing at Fairford test centre.

1969 June: Concordes 001 and 002 made first public appearance at the Paris Air Show.

1969 1 October: Concorde's first supersonic flight by 001.

1969 8 November: First airline pilots fly 001.

1969 December: Authority given for three more series production Concordes, nos 204, 205 and 206.

1970 25 March: 002 exceeded Mach 1.

1970 1 September: 002 made first flight on British West Coast test corridor.

1970 13 September: 002 appeared at SBAC Farnborough Air Show and then made first landing at an international airport, London Heathrow.

1970 4 November: 001 first achieved Mach 2.

1970 12 November: 002 first achieved Mach 2.

1971 US SST programme abandoned .

1971 April: Four more production Concordes, nos 207–210, authorised.

1971 July: Airline pilots flew at Mach 2.

1971 17 September: 001 made first automatic landing.

1971 20 September: Pre-production 01 rolled out at Filton.

1972 18 May: 1,000 Concorde flying hours logged by 001, 002 and 201.

1972 2 June: 002 departed Fairford to begin 45,000 mile sales demonstration tour of 12 countries in the Far East and Australia.

1972 BOAC ordered five Concordes followed by five by Air France.

1972 Production orders reached 16 aircraft.

1972 Government increases production loan to £350m.

1973 102, first production Concorde, made maiden flight at Toulouse.

1973 Russian Tu-144 crashed at the Paris Air Show.

1973 20 September: Concorde 002 landed at Dallas/Fort Worth on first visit to the USA.

1973 19 October: Prototype 001 was retired to French Air Museum at Le Bourget Airport after 397 flights, which covered 812 hours, 255 being at supersonic speeds.

1974 13 February: Second production Concorde (202) flew from Filton.

1974 17 June: First double Atlantic crossing in one day.

1974 12 September: 3,000 hours of flight testing achieved.

1974 21 October: 1,000 hours supersonic flying amassed by the six Concordes.

1974 An Air France Concorde flew from Boston to Paris and back, beating an Air France Boeing 747 flying from Paris to Boston one way.

1974 Pan Am and TWA dropped Concorde options.

1974 Concorde production limited to 16 aircraft.

1975 March: Draft US environmental impact statement published.

1975 November: Final US environmental impact statement published.

1975 Flight crew training began.

1975 5 December: Concorde awarded full Certificate of Airworthiness.

1976 21 January: Inauguration of commercial supersonic travel by British Airways to Bahrain.

1976 January: Air France began Paris–Rio service, via Dakar.

1976 4 February: British Airways and Air France cleared by US for each to operate two daily Concorde services to New York and one to Washington for a 16-month trial period.

1976 4 March: Concorde 002 retired to RNAS Museum at Yeovilton.

1976 11 March: Concorde banned from landing at Port Authority of New York and New Jersey airports.

1976 24 May: BA and Air France start trans-atlantic services to Washington DC.

1976 30 November: Fairford Flight Test Base closed and team returned to Filton.

1977 22 November: Inauguration of British Airways London–New York services.

1977 BA and Singapore Airlines started joint service from London to Singapore, via Bahrain.

1978 June: Concorde exempted from noise rules at New York.

1978 10 August: BA carried its 100,000th passenger on Concorde.

1978 September: BA and Air France Concorde cleared to make Cat III automatic landings.

1979 9 January: Concorde awarded United States type certificate of airworthiness.

1979 January: Braniff began a subsonic service between Washington and Fort Worth but was discontinued the following year.

1979 February: BA wrote off Concorde purchase cost.

1979 September: Unsold Concordes allocated to Air France and British Airways.

1980 British Airways received its seventh aircraft.

1980 17 June: Flights to Dallas by BA and AF ceased.

1980 1 November: BA/Singapore Airlines service discontinued.

1981 April: Commons Trade and Industry report said project 'had acquired a life of its own and was out of control'.

1981 October: Future of Concorde discussed by UK and French ministers.

1982 February: Trade and Industry Committee report reaffirmed criticism.

1982 BA Concorde Division formed. The Government handed over Concorde operations to State-owned BA, writing off development costs.

1982 Air France ceased service to Caracas and Rio.

1983 Concorde crossed the Atlantic in 2 hr 56 min.

1984 British Airways took over support costs from UK government.

1985 Concorde flew from Heathrow to Sydney in 17 hr 3 min.

1986 8 November: First round the world flight by a British Airways Concorde covering 28,238 miles in 29 hr 59 min.

1986 Concorde celebrated ten years in commercial service, with 71,000 flying hours.

1987 Scheduled London Heathrow to Barbados began.

1987 Air France took over support costs from French government.

1988 Scheduled services to Dallas Fort Worth began.

1988 G-BOAA set record flying between New York and Heathrow in 2 hr 55 min 15sec.

1988 First British Airways round the world charter.

1990 Concorde model installed at entrance to Heathrow.

1991 A new flight-planning system was introduced.

1991 BA ceased Miami service.

1992 Concorde broke the world record for fastest round the world trip in just 33 hours..

1993 BA Senior First Officer Barbara Harmer became Concorde's first female pilot.

1994 British Airways ceased Washington flights.

1995 The Ryder Cup was brought back to Europe on Concorde.

1996 7 February: Concorde made the fastest crossing of the Atlantic taking just two hours 52 minutes and 59 seconds.

1996 Life extension programme was introduced.

1997 Concorde livery changed to the Chatham Flag design.

1998 Life expansion programme was completed.

1999 11 August: Two British Airways Concordes flew in supersonic formation to chase the total eclipse of the sun over the UK.

2000 25 July: Air France Concorde F-BTSC crashed after take-off from Paris Charles de Gaulle airport with loss of all on board. Air France Concorde fleet grounded pending outcome of accident investigation.

2000 15 August: British Airways suspended its supersonic operations following the tragic accident.

2001 17 July: G-BOAF performed a supersonic verification flight, to prepare for the re-introduction to service.

2001 24 August: Air France F-BVFB flew a supersonic verification flight.

2001 5 September: Certificate of Airworthiness returned to modified Concordes by the British CAA and French DGAC.

2001 7 November: British Airways and Air France re-launched their scheduled services to New York.

2001 1 December: BA restarted Saturday-only winter service to Barbados.

2002 January: BA began major re-life programme to extend service life by six years from the then planned retirement date of 2010.

2002 4 June: Concorde flew up the Mall with the Red Arrows to celebrate The Queen's Golden Jubilee.

2003 10 April: British Airways and Air France simultaneously announced that their Concorde fleets would be retired at the end of October 2003.

2003 31 May: Air France ended scheduled Concorde services.

2003 22 June: Virgin chairman Richard Branson offered £5m to buy BA's remaining Concordes.

2003 27 June: Air France flew its last Concorde flight from Charles de Gaulle to Toulouse.

2003 30 August: BA flew its last Concorde service from Barbados.

2003 October: BA made the last flight to Toronto.

2003 8 October: BA made the last flight to Boston.

2003 14 October: BA made the last Concorde flight to Dulles, Washington.

2003 24 October: British Airways retired Concorde from commercial service with three aircraft landing consecutively at London Heathrow.

2003 26 November: Last ever flight of Concorde, when #216/G-BOAF was flown to Airbus UK at Filton for retirement.

UNITED KINGDOM
Fleet Air Arm Museum, RNAS Yeovilton, Somerset:
#002/G-BSST
Imperial War Museum, Duxford, Cambs:
#101/G-AXDN
Brooklands Museum, Weybridge, Surrey:
#202/G-BBDG
Manchester Airport Visitor Centre:
#204/G-BOAC
Scottish Museum of Flight, East Fortune:
#206/G-BOAA
London (Heathrow) Airport:
#208/G-BOAB
Airbus/Bristol Aero Collection, Filton, Bristol:
#216/G-BOAF

FRANCE
Musée de l'Air, Le Bourget, Paris:
#1/F-WTSS and #213/F-BTSD
Orly Airport, Paris:
#102/F-WTSA
Airbus Toulouse - Blagnac:
#201 F-WTSB and #209/F-BVFC
Charles de Gaulle Airport, Paris:
#215/F-BVFF

GERMANY
Auto & Technik Museum, Sinsheim:
#207/F-BVFB

USA
Steven F. Udvar-Hazy Center, Dulles Airport, Washington, DC:
#205/F-BVFA
Intrepid Sea-Air-Space Museum, New York:
#210/G-BOAD
Museum of Flight, Paine Field, Seattle, WA:
#214/G-BOAG

BARBADOS
Grantly Adams Airport, Barbados:
#212/G-BOAE

"We've got the SR-71 Blackbird, the fastest military plane ever built sitting on the flight deck, now we've got the fastest commercial airliner ever built."

Tom Tyrrell, CEO of the Intrepid Sea-Air-Space Museum in New York on receiving G-BOAD in November 2003